CREEPY PARANORMAL STORIES

A COLLECTION OF UNUSUAL ENCOUNTERS WITH HAUNTING GHOSTS AND THE UNEXPLAINED

H.J. TIDY

TABLE OF CONTENTS

INTRODUCTION

THROUGHOUT THE AGES, individuals from diverse backgrounds and eras have remained captivated by the mysterious and unexplainable. From ancient civilizations to contemporary enthusiasts, the magnetic allure of the paranormal endures. "Creepy Paranormal Stories" invites you to embark on a captivating journey through the enigmatic realm of the supernatural.

This book doesn't seek to impose any beliefs on you but rather to take you on a voyage into the mysterious and unexplainable. Within these pages, you'll encounter various strange and unconventional stories. Whether you choose to believe some or all of them is entirely up to you, as these tales are sure to captivate even the most skeptical readers.

As we embark on this exploration of the dark and enigmatic, let's delve into the recurring themes, individuals, and emotions that thread through these paranormal narratives. Whether we confront unexplained phenomena or a belief in sinister forces, unsettling occurrences within family homes that prompt midnight escapes, or the mysteries surrounding strange deaths and perplexing disappearances, the supernatural and the unexplained leave an indelible mark on our minds and souls. These stories blur the line between the natural world and enduring enigmas, challenging the boundaries of reason and the supernatural.

The characters in these tales offer unique perspectives and experiences that add an extra layer of intrigue. Consider Anna Ecklund's story, a testament to her remarkable ability to transform and endure despite life's trials. Known initially as Emma Schmidt, Anna faced a challenging upbringing and displayed troubling behaviors. Her encounter with evil forces forced her to grapple with inner turmoil. Yet, she managed to lead a more ordinary life after this traumatic event, demonstrating her resilience and achieving a sense of stability and peace.

Similarly, the case of Jackie Hernandez in the peculiar episode in San Pedro reveals a notable transformation as she endured a series of paranormal events in her new home and sought assistance from paranormal investigators to restore normalcy to her life. This highlights the power of human resilience and emotional healing in the face of traumatic events.

From Anna Ecklund's confrontation with the supernatural to Jackie Hernandez's unwavering emotional strength, we witness the potential for personal transformation, spiritual growth, and enlightenment amidst the challenges presented by the paranormal. The emotions evoked in these chronicles span a broad spectrum, from the heart-wrenching fear and torment experienced by Bill Vaile as he grapples with unexplained supernatural occurrences.

In the Headless Valley, the accounts of tragic fatalities and mysterious disappearances instill a palpable sense of trepidation. At the same time, the legend of the Waheela adds an element of strange mystery to an already peculiar setting. Please be aware that these tales are not for the faint of heart. Some may be unsettling and disturbing. Reader discretion is advised.

These tales serve as a testament to the potency of paranormal narratives in igniting curiosity and connecting us through our shared fascination with the unexplained. Take a moment to immerse yourself in these uncanny chronicles and contemplate the lasting emotions and profound concepts they conjure.

So, turn on a light, get comfortable, and prepare for a thrilling journey through these "Creepy Paranormal Stories."

1

VALLEY OF THE HEADLESS PEOPLE

THE NAHANNI VALLEY, OR NAHANNI NATIONAL PARK RESERVE, is in the Northwest Territories in Canada and is part of the Dehcho Region. This area of land is rich with history, dating back to the records of the First Nations people who originated there. The land is also fraught with supernatural tales. A wild and unpredictable area, the Nahanni Valley is home to many of the most intriguing encounters in Canada.

This chapter encompasses the experiences of many people who have visited the Nahanni Valley. From the horrible ordeal of the native people to search parties looking for missing persons decades later, this region has been unforgiving to humans and animals alike for a very long time.

What is the Nahanni Valley?

The Nahanni Valley is part of an expansive strip of inhospitable land: The Northern Territories, with is a mostly undisturbed part of the world. The region is packed with thick, dense forests, enormous mountains, large waterfalls, deep river canyons, and lakes. This natural landscape is beautiful, but untamed. Additionally, wild animals roam here, including large black bears, mountain goats, deer, and even grizzly bears. This poses yet another danger to any people who visit. In the middle of it all is the Nahanni Valley, which stretches over approximately eleven thousand square meters and is perhaps the most hazardous region within the entire Northern Territories. Because of this, it is rare to find anybody living there. Even for the most experienced outdoors people, it can be a dangerous and unlivable place.

Despite how dangerous it can be, the valley was declared a national park in 1976 by UNESCO and inscribed on the World Heritage List in 1978 to protect the region (UNESCO World Heritage Centre, 2021). Over time, further land has been added to the national park to protect the picturesque and unique landscape. It is important to note that this is no ordinary national park. It is not a place that families can visit for a picnic; it has no tourist accommodations and no roads lead into the park. It is primarily accessible by either plane, boat, or a very challenging hike that is not for the faint of heart. Due to its remote nature, the valley remains one of the most untouched national parks in Northern America and represents nature in its purest form.

While the land itself is treacherous, it is not the only reason people are hesitant to visit. This valley is said to be haunted. Many people have experienced extreme trauma throughout its history, making it even more enticing and even more dangerous.

The Deaths in the Valley

First Nations People, Disappearances, and Waheela

The Nahanni Valley is home to the indigenous tribe named the Dene, which translates to "The People Over There". Over the last ten thousand years, many other tribes have attempted to settle here, though only a few have been successful. This is theorized to be because of the harsh climate; however, there may also be a paranormal element.

First Nations people use oral history to relay their stories through the generations, and one such story is that of the disappearing tribes in the valley. The Naha tribe was one of these, and one of the strangest stories from this region. The tale says this tribe vanished completely, without a trace. All their supplies were abandoned, including shelter, food, and goods. Nobody knows what happened to them, and there is no knowledge of their current whereabouts.

Other tribes have attempted to settle but have had to flee from the land abruptly due to strange dangers presenting themselves. Some reported seeing a "white demon" lurking in the woods and feared that it would attack them. Some tribesmen described this creature as an incredibly large white wolf and named it Waheela. This wolf is said to rip heads off humans and be a supernatural creature inhabited by a demon. Skeptics have dismissed this as folklore, but this has not stopped many from believing that the Waheela stalk the valley's forests.

The McLeod Brothers, Robert Weir, and the Headless Valley

During the North American gold rushes, three brothers—Frank, Willie, and Charlie McLeod—looked for their fortune in the Nahanni Valley in 1904. The brothers were originally from the Northwest Territories and felt equipped to venture into this region. Their journey was not an easy one. They used many means to make their way through, including sled dogs and handmade boats. They eventually reached the Flat River, which runs through the middle of the Nahanni Valley. The name of the Flat River is an ironic one, as it is anything but flat. There are steep rapids throughout, many of which are unexpected and dangerous.

Nonetheless, the brothers persevered and set up camp alongside the riverbank to pan for gold. Right away, they were successful and spent all day and night collecting gold. The next day, they decided to go home and sell their findings, planning to make their way back to the valley later. To do this, they decided to traverse the river on their boat. This was, unfortunately, a very dangerous idea. Their boat was broken by the powerful rapids, and the gold they had collected caused the remnants to sink. The brothers grabbed what they could of their supplies and swam to shore, losing their fortune. They fashioned another boat shortly after and returned to where they previously struck gold, but were ultimately unsuccessful the second time. They left, but the two younger brothers, Willie and Frank, planned to return to the valley, confident that they would find the gold once more.

In 1905, the two brothers decided it was time to make the voyage again. The oldest, Charlie, felt it was too dangerous, so they replaced him with their friend Robert Weir to make up a three-person team. The men decided they would set up camp in the valley long-term, and did not indicate when they would return. However, friends and family grew concerned after months of no contact. Charlie initially eased these concerns. He believed his brothers and friend had simply struck gold again and were busy collecting. However, Charlie's opinion changed when the men had not been heard from in two years. Finally, the oldest brother set up a search party to find them.

The search party that Charlie established made the arduous journey into the Nahanni Valley and made their way to the Flat River, finding no sign of the men. They broke off into groups, some searching the larger South Nahanni River and others searching upstream to find some clue as to their whereabouts. The South Nahanni River is yet another treacherous part of the valley. The river is about 350 miles long and has four canyons. These canyons are enormous sheer cliffs on both sides of the riverbed, and they rise up to three thousand feet above the water. There is nowhere to go other than down the canyon and into the terrifying water.

To get to a shoreline, one must get through this section of the river and then off their boat and go on foot. Along this shoreline, there are massive openings that lead to a vast cave system that is almost impossible to navigate. Traditionally, people know not to go into the caves as there is no knowing what is inside them. Whether you believe in the supernatural or not, dangerous animals still reside in the forest and often take shelter in these caves. Another dangerous of the river lies nearby, with a 45-degree turn at one point resulting in a ten-mile stretch called the Second Canyon. Only when the search party ventured into this deep and dangerous Second Canyon did they find a tent perched on the shoreline.

They moved to inspect the tent, and as they approached they saw a body lying on the ground, missing its head. As they surveyed the area, they found another body at the back of the camping area, which was also missing its head and was severely decomposed. Initially, the party could not establish the identity of the two bodies. Upon further investigation, they found personal items belonging to Frank and Willie nearby. It was likely that these bodies were those of the McLeod brothers. Robert Weir was not located, nor were the heads of the two deceased men. In later years, a skeleton that was found that is believed to be that of Robert Weir, though this is unconfirmed.

Charlie McLeod and his search party reached out to the police, who would launch an investigation into the brothers' deaths. While the police concluded the men starved to death and that any signs of mutilation came postmortem from animals, Charlie believed it was native tribes who had attacked them. He had found an inscription on a tree near the campsite, which read "we have found a fine prospect", and believed his brothers were murdered for the gold they had found. There was no gold at their campsite, and he proposed it had been stolen. Another theory was that Robert attacked the brothers for their share of the gold and had left them for dead, disappearing into the forest alone and eventually meeting his demise. People who knew the history of the valley believed it was the work of the Waheela, due to the decapitation of the bodies.

The news of the headless men in the Nahanni Valley spread quickly, and people became even more hesitant to make the voyage into the dangerous forest. The second canyon where the men were found was renamed Headless Valley, and even the prospect of gold was not enough for people to risk their lives in such a terrifying location.

Martin Jorgensen

Despite the terrifying history of the Nahanni Valley, gold prospector Martin Jorgensen decided to try his luck in the valley all on his own. In 1913, less than ten years after the death of the McLeod brothers, Martin began his voyage and found a spot to settle approximately fifty miles upstream from Headless Valley. Martin decided to stay over the winter, so he built himself a one-room cabin to live in. He planned to have his partners visit over the summer and even sent word that he had found gold, advising that this would make them rich. Sadly, this was the last time anybody heard from Martin Jorgensen.

When the summer came, Martin's partners arrived in the Nahanni Valley, looking for their friend. They found his cabin burned to the ground and a headless body belonging to Martin next to the cabin. Once again, the police were called to investigate; however, they never formally linked this death to the McLeod brothers. They were unable to determine the cause of death and theorized that it was an animal attack. Unfortunately, just like Frank and Willie, the skull was never found. Nor was the gold that Martin had collected.

John O'Brien

By 1921, tales from the Nahanni Valley were well known. Some believed a serial killer was loose in the forest, while others firmly believed the cause of the deaths was paranormal. Nonetheless, this did not stop gold prospector John O'Brien and his partner from roaming into the belly of the beast. The two men set up in the Headless Valley and found gold, just like those who had come before them.

One day, John left his partner to check traps set along the river and was never seen alive again. After approximately nine days, his partner became concerned and reached out to another gold prospector he knew in the area to assist him in finding John. Unfortunately, the two men came upon his body, frozen to death. Those who saw John's body noted that he was positioned oddly. He was found sitting in front of a campfire, holding a matchbook in his hands. Some believe that he may have experienced the phenomenon of being flash-frozen, as though it happened in seconds and he barely had time to react before freezing to death. Despite the strange circumstances around his death, the police ruled it an accident, and no further investigation took place. However, those who believed in the supernatural and cursed nature of the Nahanni Valley couldn't help but see this as further proof that something was afoot in the forest.

Annie Lafferty

Five years later, in 1926, a hunting party entered the Headless Valley. This party included Annie Lafferty, who went missing one night without a trace. The hunting party immediately looked for her, but could not find a single clue where she went. They contacted the police, and an extensive search was organized, but Annie was never found.

Several months later, a man named Charlie came forward with information about her. He said he was near the hunting party on the night she went missing, but was not a part of the group. He heard that a woman had gone missing but did not join the search and remained in his camp. That very night, the sound of rocks falling into the river he was camping beside woke him, and he went to investigate the sound. He exited his tent into a dark night illuminated only by the light of the moon. He saw a woman upon a huge rock, standing on all fours and completely naked. Her movements caused smaller rocks to fall into the river. Charlie was able to get close enough to see her face, and was terrified because she looked as though she was possessed. He did not follow her and did not feel safe enough to go near this woman. When he saw a photo of Annie, he told the police that it was the same woman he saw that night.

There is no evidence to support this story, as Annie was never found, but some people believe that a supernatural being possessed this young woman.

Death by Fire

Just four years later, in 1931, Phil Powers wanted to find gold for himself. He camped in the Headless Valley, built a cabin, and intended to stay there indefinitely. Before long, his cabin mysteriously burned to the ground and his skeleton was found intact. It is suspected that Phil died before the fire started, though it is unclear how the blaze began.

In 1936, William Eppler and Joseph Mulholland experienced similar fates, with their cabin also found burned to the ground. However, unlike Phil, their bodies were never found.

John Patterson

In 1946, yet another tragedy happened in the Headless Valley. John Patterson was another gold prospector seeking riches who unfortunately went missing like those before him. A party searched the Headless Valley and camped by the river. They were approached by First Nations people offering information: They witnessed white figures lurking in the valley and claimed they were seen both by the river and in the forest. They warned those in the camp to be careful and advised that they needed to steer clear of these figures.

That night, the search party heard howls and screams echoing around them, though they were unsure of the source of the sound. They thought perhaps the natives were trying to scare them and make them leave. If that was the goal, they were successful. The party packed up their camp and were gone by the following day. Their sudden exit meant that John Patterson was never found, and many of the search party members were scarred forever by the sounds they heard that night.

What is Really Happening at the Nahanni Valley?

Since the 1940s, reports of strange happenings in the Nahanni Valley have decreased. This could be because people are less inclined to visit, as word of the dangers and deaths in the valley has spread far and wide. More recently, certain parts of the park have been closed to the public to preserve wildlife sections. However, many believe those sections have been closed to protect any potential visitors from the horrors that lurk inside the forest.

What is really happening at the Nahanni Valley? Is the Headless Valley the stomping ground for demons, or were the many deaths that occurred there purely accidental? Unfortunately, the true answer remains a mystery. Those who believe in the paranormal think that the Nahanni Valley is haunted and that the deaths and missing people are due to demons and spirits. They see the beheadings as the works of the mythic Waheela and that the flash freezing of John O'Brien and the supposed possession of Annie Lafferty could only be the works of the supernatural. They also point to the random fires that have killed many people as the unexplainable work of the paranormal.

Skeptics, however, believe that the stories of the Nahanni Valley are purely folklore. They think that the deaths were accidental, often due to natural causes and animals, and that the valley is only dangerous because it is wild and untamed. Some also believe that unknown native tribes have attacked visitors; however, these claims are entirely unfounded.

It is truly up to the individual to draw a conclusion on what they believe is happening in this terrifying part of the world. No matter what you believe, there is no denying that the Nahanni Valley is a dangerous, intriguing place, and quite assuredly not safe to visit.

2

THE PECULIAR CASE IN SAN PEDRO

SAN PEDRO, IN LOS ANGELES, CALIFORNIA, is considered a relatively safe place to live. It is close to the water, has a low crime rate, and boasts one of the busiest ports in the United States. It is also where Jackie Hernandez moved to with her young son in 1989.

Unfortunately for Jackie, this move did not provide the peace she was seeking. Rather, it resulted in a severe case of paranormal activity. Jackie claims to have been haunted in this home and experienced the ghosts of vengeful spirits who sought to torture her. Like any famous haunting story, many skeptics do not believe Jackie's story, though it is difficult to deny that something strange happened in this home.

Jackie Moves to San Pedro

In 1989, at the age of twenty-three, Jackie Hernandez left her husband, Al. The couple had been unhappy for some time. Even though she was pregnant with their second child, she took their son, Jamie, and moved away. She hoped to find a little bit of peace away from her marriage. Instead, Jackie entered one of the most terrifying paranormal stories in recent history and found anything but the quiet she was looking for.

Jackie and Jamie settled into their new home, a bungalow in the suburb of San Pedro. Initially, they were happy with their fresh start, and there was nothing suspect or unusual about their lives there.

This would soon change. Jackie's first sign that something strange was happening in the house came from a sound in the walls, which sounded like little pebbles falling, though this was not enough to cause major concern. During this time, Jackie also had her second child, Samantha, born in April 1989 (Abrams, 1993). She reported that this was when the paranormal experiences took over the house.

Jackie and her family soon began to hear unexplained footsteps in the attic. At first, she brushed this off as just the normal noises of an old home. But when her friend Susan visited one night, a loud bang came from the kitchen. Upon inspection, Jackie and Susan found a picture frame had fallen, though they couldn't understand why.

Strangely, the nails that held the frame were sitting neatly upright next to the picture, and it made no sense that the frame would fall on its own. However, for Jackie Hernandez, this was just the beginning of the strange things that would happen in her home.

Terrifying Encounters

Little did Jackie know that the photo falling was the start of something much bigger. The next night, a babysitter visited the house. Her name was Tina Lawler, and she was about to have a paranormal experience that would forever change her perspective on the supernatural. Tina went to check on the children, but before she could open the door, it drifted open on its own. She didn't think this was unusual at the time and completed her check of the children, who were sleeping soundly. Then, she shut the door behind her. Again, it opened on its own. Although slightly unnerved, Tina again didn't think much of this.

The next night, Tina returned to the house. While in the kitchen with Jackie, Tina noticed a light in the corner of the kitchen that she had not seen the day before. She asked Jackie if she had a new light installed and pointed at it. Jackie had no idea what the light was, and they noticed it was moving. The two women took a picture of this as proof that something strange was happening. This was the point where Jackie knew they were experiencing something abnormal. Tina experienced another incident alone, where a candle burning in the house fell onto some sheets. When she put out the flame, a face was burned into the sheet it had landed on. However, the rest of the sheet was intact with no sign of damage, and just the terrifying face remained.

Jackie took the photograph of the light to her ex-husband. She hoped Al could help her figure out what was happening in the house. Al, a skeptic of the paranormal, didn't believe Jackie, but could see that she was panicked. They decided the only thing they could do to resolve the situation was call out the spirit. Jackie didn't want him to do this, worried this would cause worse problems, but nothing happened when he challenged the ghost to reveal itself. After Al left the house, Jackie was doing some chores and opened her closet door, where she found writing in red and blue all over the closet, spelling out Al's name written multiple times. She believed that this was retaliation for calling the spirit, and a reaction to Al entering the home.

Other things happened after this incident. Another friend, Kristina Zivkovic, was washing dishes in the kitchen when it appeared the house were bleeding as a red liquid oozed from the walls, only to disappear as soon as it appeared. Voices were frequently heard in the house, and things would randomly move. Jackie also saw a figure in the house of an angry man who seemed to want to hurt her. She was thrown from her bed by him and often saw him in mirrors in the house. She felt as though she was going crazy.

Jackie was terrified for her safety and confided in Susan, telling her that she would move if she had the financial means, but this was not an option for her. Jackie reached out to her landlord and advised him of the happenings, hoping that he would understand. Luckily, he was a religious man and was concerned about the claims. He arranged for two priests to visit the home, and Jackie agreed to this.

When the priests arrived, they were shocked at the state of the house, finding disarray and mess. The children were crying, and Jackie seemed very stressed. They assessed the home and found nothing to explain why this was happening, which provided no resolution for Jackie. The priests filed a complaint with Child Protective Services (CPS) against Jackie, worried for the safety of the children. They believed that Jackie could have been hallucinating and was perhaps an unfit mother due to the state of the home. CPS advised Jackie that they would do checks on her and that she needed to clean up the place, and she agreed to these terms. This was when Jackie and her kids started sleeping in the same room, her fear of both the paranormal and losing her children compounding into the worst experience of her life. She had to do something.

A Paranormal Investigation

Jackie Hernandez decided to call in the help of Barry Taff, a parapsychologist who would investigate the house. A friend of Jackie's had seen Barry on television and recommended she call him. It took little convincing for her to do so. She was desperate and needed somebody in the house who would both believe and help her. At this stage, Taff had three thousand paranormal cases behind him and felt he knew the difference between what was real and what wasn't. The *LA Times* quotes him saying, "The majority of cases aren't worth pursuing. There's a lot of fabrication, a lot of invention, a lot of embellishment, and a lot of outright fraud" (Abrams, 1993). While he wasn't sure what was happening at the Hernandez home, the case intrigued him greatly.

Taff called in three additional investigators to help him with the case. On August 8th, 1989, they entered the home and began their exploration. They came prepared; they brought "sophisticated video cameras, image intensifiers, infrared detectors, and other equipment that might capture images of the unknown" (Abrams, 1993). They would cover all bases. While in the house, Taff recalls hearing something in the attic, which he described to be similar to a two-hundred-pound rat. He also felt overpressure, which he described as the sensation of being underwater. Additionally, he reported the smells of a haunting, which he recognized from his years in the field.

The most terrifying experience for the paranormal team was in the attic, where Jackie and visitors had often heard noises. Upon entering this space, the team photographer, Jeff Wheatcraft, was holding his camera. This was torn from him and thrown across the room. They later found the lens several feet away from the rest of the camera. When they returned the next day, Jeff was once again the target of the supernatural. This time, he was attacked with a clothesline wrapped around his neck, then the spirit attempted to hang him from a protruding nail (Abrams, 1993).

The team took video evidence of Jeff hanging from the nail, and the video showed objects being moved by invisible figures and light orbs that streaked the camera. Taff saw this as proof that something paranormal was happening. He also noted that this was a particularly volatile spirit, and that there was likely more than one ghost in the house. Jackie had seen an older man, but there was also evidence of a younger. He also commented that he had never seen a spirit be so violent towards the investigators. "In the whole history of the paranormal... there have been a handful of cases, maybe five cases, where people have been harmed or injured... This is the first case I've ever been on where the phenomenon went after the researchers" (Abrams, 1993).

Who Was the Ghost Haunting Jackie?

Jackie and Al attempted to reconcile their marriage, and Jackie and the kids moved from the haunted property. Unfortunately, things fell apart again after a few months, and Jackie's life was in turmoil. At this time, the haunting also returned. It seemed whenever Jackie was in emotional distress, the spirit would appear, though she did not make this correlation at the time.

The occurrences were different at this time, though they were still unsettling.

While moving a television with some neighbors, the screen turned on and showed the face of a man that Jackie recognized as the man from the San Pedro house. The television was moved into a shed. That night, the sound of someone banging in the shed woke Jackie, sounding like someone wanting to get out. Once again, she engaged the help of paranormal investigators, except this time they couldn't capture any footage, as something kept switching off the devices.

Once again, the photographer was violently targeted and thrown into the wall by an invisible entity.

After this, they decided to try a Ouija board, which might give Jackie the answers she needed about what was haunting her. A transcript of the interaction provides the details of one spirit. First, the spirit identified that he had not died in the San

Pedro home, but was murdered by the person who had once lived there. He was drowned by a man in the San Pedro Bay in 1930 at age 18.

Further investigation found this man could have been Herman Hendrickson, a seaman who died in March 1930. However, inconsistencies emerged. First, Herman was about ten years older than the conversation with the Ouija board indicated, and he died from a wound to the neck, not drowning, though he fell from the dock. This meant the Ouija board ghost remained unnamed. However, there were at least two ghosts suspected to be in the home, because the ghost Jackie had reported was an older man. Jackie believed that this man was John Damon, the original builder of the bungalow, who had died at an elderly age.

In the spring of 1990, the ghost believed to be John left Jackie for good. She recalls it being a peaceful departure. First, he appeared to her as a ball of light. When she followed this light, she found herself at the gravestone of John Damon, and the light hovered over this stone, then disappeared (Abrams, 1993). Finally, Jackie's living hell was over.

Skeptics and Believers

The *LA Times* opens their article on this incident by saying, "File this one under maybe. Big on the maybe" (Abrams, 1993). Skeptics of this case are sure that Jackie Hernandez was not haunted, but was going through some sort of psychosis or mental breakdown due to the end of her marriage. This hypothesis is supported by the fact that when she reunited with her husband, the haunting stopped, and it only started back up again after their marriage ended for good. The situation also got worse after she feared losing her children, with the integrity of the spirit's behavior directly correlating with her emotional state. They also believe the paranormal investigators fabricated evidence to make the situation seem worse, seeking financial gain from the story they produced. Barry Taff was already on television, and some believe that this was just going to be another way that he would cash in on the fear of the paranormal.

However, the evidence is quite damning that something was happening at the house. First, Jackie wasn't the only person who witnessed the spirit, so the argument that this was a psychotic break is poor. A handful of friends and a babysitter attested to her claims before the paranormal investigators were ever called, so how could this have been all in her head? Second, there is physical evidence by the investigators that shows the supernatural happening. Taff himself admits that not everybody will believe this, though it does not make him believe any less. "The problem is that today, anything can be faked. It's not truth beyond a reasonable doubt" (Abrams, 1993).

Jackie has stood by her claims and is positive that a ghost was haunting her. There was likely more than one ghost living in the home, and then a spirit latched to her when she moved, only appearing when she was vulnerable. This coincides with lore involving spirits, as the emotionally fragile and vulnerable are often targets for this kind of activity. Regardless of what you believe, or whether you think Jackie is telling the truth, this remains a fascinating story.

The house itself has become somewhat of a feature of the suburb of San Pedro, with children visiting on Halloween and many believing that it is still haunted to this day (ABC7, 2009). Since Jackie and her children moved from the home, there have been reports of more paranormal experiences at the property, but none as violent and terrifying as that of the Hernandez family.

3

THE EXORCISM OF ANNA ECKLUND

THE STORY OF ANNA ECKLUND IS ONE OF THE MOST FAMOUS, well-documented exorcism cases in US history. Her story is harrowing, involving a horrendous demonic possession and two horrible attempts at an exorcism. Anna suffered so greatly from her affliction that movies have been made about her experience since her death, and books have been written detailing what she went through. Her story will not be quickly forgotten.

Who Was Anna?

Anna Ecklund is the pseudonym of Emma Schmidt, who is more often than not known as Anna. She is also sometimes known as Mary X, as this was the name recorded at her birth. She was born in 1882 in Wisconsin to German immigrants. Her parents were highly devout Catholics and raised their daughter to follow in their footsteps. Unfortunately, Anna's mother died when she was eight, leaving her in the care of her father. He was known to be a violent alcoholic and abused Anna. It is believed that he also sexually abused her, and when she refuted him, his anger at this led to more violence.

Despite the horrors of her childhood, Anna remained a devout Catholic herself, attending church whenever given the opportunity and engaging with her community through religious activities. By all accounts, Anna was a well-behaved young girl dedicated to God and the church.

Anna did not speak openly about the abuse in her household; however, she may have told her aunt Mina, who lived nearby. Anna's relationship with this aunt is unclear; but some have theorized that Mina was also her father's lover and did not believe the claims. Others have said that the aunt was practicing black magic against Anna to get rid of the girl. While this is just speculation, it is interesting that the one person who may have known about the abuse not only did nothing to help, but may have been conspiring against her.

The Changes Begin

It was between the ages of ten and fourteen that Anna seemed to change into a different person. As a young girl so dedicated to religion, it is no surprise that her changing attitude towards God was her first clue that something was wrong with her. For starters, Anna began to experience revulsion toward religious artifacts that had once brought her comfort and solace, like a cross to ward off evil spirits or her beloved bible. She could not stand the sight of them anymore. She sometimes even felt compelled to destroy them, feeling violent in a way she had never experienced before. She felt uneasy when entering a church, flooded with unsavory and uncomfortable thoughts at crossing the threshold, and felt uncomfortable during sermons. By fourteen, she started missing church, unable to stand those feelings. She also claimed that something was telling her not to go to church. Overall, Anna became very distant from the community that had once been her whole life, seemingly forsaking the beliefs she held most dear.

Anna also began to hear voices and could not control what was happening in her mind. The voice that told her not to go to church was only getting louder, and her violent outbursts against religious artifacts became more common. She was unable to control her thoughts or behaviors, and was terrified of what was happening to her.

It could be that Anna's disdain for religion

came as a psychological response to the abuse she was experiencing at the hands of her father. Around this time, the sexual abuse had allegedly begun. Regardless of the real reasoning, those who knew her became very concerned with what was happening to her and thought that a demonic possession may have changed the young girl.

Taking Action

At first, Anna was taken to a doctor to discuss the changes and issues she was facing. Over a few months, Anna saw many doctors, none of whom could diagnose her with anything or help her with the mental and physical issues she was facing. Anna's thoughts and behaviors were violent and out of her control, and she was becoming more and more scared of her growing disdain towards the church and religion. She had changed so drastically from the young girl who reveled in being a church community member. She had always found solace in her religious beliefs, and found it extremely difficult to reconcile that the thing which bought her joy was causing her pain. Besides all her other symptoms, Anna had intrusive sexual thoughts that disturbed her greatly. Reportedly, these intensified around churches and religious artifacts, and were the last straw before she felt she could no longer live with this condition. When her visits to various doctors turned up no results, Anna was connected with Father Theophilus Riesinger.

Father Riesinger was a German priest who

immigrated to the United States, similar to Anna's parents. After practicing in New York, he moved to the Midwest and met Anna that year. It is speculated that Anna's father was the first person to accuse her of demonic possession. After she refused his sexual advances, their relationship was almost non-existent and he showed no care for the wellbeing of his daughter. Another possibility is that Anna's aunt Mina advised Father Riesinger of this potential possession to aid Anna's father in his vendetta against her. Regardless of who came to the priest with the information, he soon deemed that Anna's change in behavior could only be blamed on the devil, and sought to perform an exorcism on her. Unfortunately, there is not much detail about the first exorcism, only that it seemed successful and allowed Anna to return to a normal life. After this, Father Theophilus Riesinger became a well-known exorcism expert, and the frequency at which he performed them heightened.

The Second Possession

Anna's life remained normal for the next two decades. Her father died, and with him, so did the abuse she was facing. She grew out of her teenage years and into a woman with her past just a bad memory. This was until 1928, when Anna's intrusive and aggressive thoughts returned. This time, Anna was completely unable to control her thoughts. She hated religion, feeling violent towards the church and those affiliated with it. She fell into despair, unsure of why this was happening to her again. With her father long dead, she was no longer being abused by him, and she had long moved on from her old life.

People circulated rumors that her Aunt Mina was once again responsible, as she had become known as a witch who practiced dark magic, but Anna had no communication with her. She was desperate for answers and for a way to regain control of her life. With no way of resolving her problem, Anna once again turned to the church. The Bishop of the Diocese of Des Moines learned of her issues and past demonic possession, and called for Father Theophilus Riesinger. Once again, Father Riesinger was asked to perform an exorcism on Anna Ecklund; except this time, the experience would be far better documented and far more horrifying.

Father Riesinger believed the demons inside Anna had doubled up and would be much harder to expel. He could not use the same methods as before, as it would be much tougher to save Anna's soul. He was convinced he would have a fight on his hands if he didn't go into the exorcism with full force. He believed it would be best to isolate Anna before and during the exorcism, and sought permission from the mother superior of a local convent to bring her to them. The Franciscan sisters agreed to take her on, and on August 17, 1928, Anna began to live in the convent.

As Anna's main triggers seemed to be religion,

this only intensified her issues. Religious artifacts and symbolism constantly surrounded her, and she felt herself going mad while confined there. She attacked the nuns and rejected the food and drink that they bought her. She knew the food had been blessed, and was therefore unable to eat it. The nuns also claimed she had an unexplainable knowledge of what had contact with holy water and what hadn't. In the presence of any food that had touched the holy water, Anna would hiss and snarl until the nuns took it away. Anna sat in her room for hours on end, and the nuns claimed to have heard her purring to herself as she awaited Father Riesinger. Even before the exorcism started, Anna experienced a life of torture.

On August 18, 1928, the first day of the exorcism began. Father Riesinger identified that Anna's was the worst case of demonic possession he had ever witnessed and knew it would be a long ordeal. He performed the exorcism over twenty-three days, in three separate sessions. The first of the sessions lasted eight days, ending on August 26. The nuns assisted Father Riesinger in tying Anna into restraints, as she was increasingly violent during the exorcisms. He was afraid she would harm him or herself. There was no way of knowing how she would react once a session began.

As the priest chanted in Latin during the session, Anna responded by snarling back in the same language as though her mouth were not her own. Anna never learned Latin, and could have no idea how to speak it. Sometimes her retorts would be so passionate and aggressive she would foam at the mouth. Anna would also speak in German, another language she had not previously known. At times, she would seemingly lay unconscious during the exorcisms. Then all of a sudden, a noise would emerge from her, speaking in otherworldly tongues, Latin, or German. Then a beast-like growl would be heard before the noise would stop again. Anna would remain asleep, her eyes and mouth both shut as this happened, but the sound was undeniably coming from her.

Anna could not eat or drink anything in the days leading up to the exorcism. Yet during the session, she would foam at the mouth and vomit an incomprehensible amount. She would vomit up substances she had not touched, like tobacco leaves and spices that she had been nowhere near. While she reportedly only managed a teaspoon or so of milk and water in the hours before her sessions, she would end up vomiting incredibly large amounts of fluids, more than any human should be able to expel. The smell was so horrendous that the nuns were unable to stand it. The same smell appeared in Anna's room in the convent, and the nuns often found it so disgusting they couldn't bring themselves to clean it right away.

The first session came to a close with everyone involved needing to break from the horrors. It was also important for Anna to recuperate before the next session started, as this was particularly grueling for her. They began again on September 13, and this session would last the next seven days. Anna's behavior only worsened during this time. It is reported that she would perform otherworldly acts, the likes of which had never been seen before. For example, Anna would levitate, breaking free of her shackles to float in the air. Sometimes, her body became so heavy that she would sink completely into the bed, breaking the iron frame and legs. There was no explanation how a small woman could cause this much destruction. Anna's physical being also transformed. Her skin became red and swollen until it seemed she was about to burst. From this, she would quickly become white and frail, looking as though she were completely starved. She would switch from one extreme to another with no apparent trigger.

Anna continued to abuse those in the convent verbally and would allow nobody to help her. She also recited the sins of any visitor or person she came across, sins that these people had never confessed. She had somehow gained intimate knowledge of secrets that the nuns and priests had told nobody. Further to that, the stench in her room became so disgusting that those who had to enter could only stay briefly. Along with the smell, the room felt like a pit of darkness.

Before entering the exorcism sessions, Father Riesinger attended mass along with any assisting priests, the pastor, and the nuns at the convent.

Then they would all arm themselves with various religious objects before heading to Anna's room. On one occasion, as soon as the priest began reciting the Holy Trinity, Anna broke through her restraints, fought off the nuns who were assisting, and leaped sideways onto the wall before climbing up it. While doing this, she was snarling like an animal. Everything about this incident reminded those who witnessed it of something nonhuman.

After this, on September 20, Father Riesinger called the second session to a break, fearing that he was endangering not just Anna's life but also those around her. Anna was changing so drastically during these sessions that those around her worried she would be lost forever. Father Reisinger thought perhaps the demon inside Anna was too angry at him, as he had a long history with her at this stage. He asked for the help of a fellow priest, Father Stagger, who he wanted to take over the sessions. Though he would still assist, he thought it would be best for someone else to lead the charge, as at that stage, nothing was helping. Father Reisinger concluded that Anna had not one but five demons inside of her. He believed them to be her father, her aunt, Beelzebub, Judas, and Lucifer. He believed Lucifer was leading the charge against him as he remembered the previous exorcism.

The third and final session began on December 15. Immediately, Father Stagger found it very difficult to lead the exorcism. He felt as though he were under personal attack and would not attend every session, though he would assist where he could. Father Issachar also began to assist, but would not lead them. This put Father Reisinger back into the leadership position as they attempted to help Anna. Throughout the sessions, they asked the demons why they were assailing her, and a voice that claimed to be Judas anwered, saying they would bring Anna so much despair that she would have no choice but to kill herself.

On December 22, those assisting the exorcism had a phenomenal breakthrough. As Anna levitated from the bed, Father Issachar screamed out and demanded that all the demons return to hell. As this happened, they saw a vision of the room filling with fire and in the corner of the room, the demons Judas and Beelzebub. Father Riesinger claimed he saw the demons filled with rage as they could not harm the priests, and saw that Lucifer had also appeared, describing him as a tall presence with matted black fur and a hoofed lower body. Anna's voice reached highest pitch it had ever hit, and a horrendous stench rushed through the room.

After this episode, Anna's eyes opened and she spoke in her own voice for the first time in months. After three exorcism sessions, the evil had left her body, and she was free of the demons that had tormented her life for so long.

Every nun who had been there during the exorcism requested a transfer. They could not stand being at this convent with the memories of what they had witnessed overwhelming them.

Father Theophilus Riesinger recorded the details of this exorcism on a pamphlet he titled *"Begone Satan"*, as he wanted to show how Satan's powers could work to the next generation of seminary students. Thus, he became the most famous exorcist of his time.

What Really Happened to Anna?

In the years after her exorcism, Anna Ecklund lived a normal life. She was no longer plagued with intrusive and violent thoughts and no longer exhibited any signs of demonic possession. It appeared her long and arduous four months with Father Riesinger in the covenant had been worth it. She was in good health and happy spirits for the remainder of her days. She died in 1941 at age fifty-nine.

While the argument for demonic possession is strong, it is also likely that Anna Ecklund was experiencing a mental illness or psychological episode that caused her to act in this way. For those who do not believe in things such as exorcisms, this is an obvious conclusion. Her case can be likened to Anneliese Michel's, a young girl in Germany who died after an attempted exorcism in 1976.

Thanks studies of Anneliese's case, it has been proposed that those who have been accused of demonic possession actually suffered from autoimmune encephalitis, also known as brain on fire disease. The neuroscience department at

Monash University describes this disease as "when your body attacks your brain, and people think you're going mad. It's described as feeling like your brain is on fire. People with autoimmune encephalitis (AE) are often misdiagnosed as suffering from a psychiatric illness, delirium, or dementia" (Monif, 2020). The disease can make you believe many things are true, including that the devil possesses you. This is a credible theory of what happened to both Anneliese and Anna. It is also possible that Anna's history of abuse triggered a psychotic break in her, which caused her to experience a deep psychosis.

While these theories are interesting, it is impossible to ignore the first-hand accounts of what Anna went through during her exorcism. She displayed many inhumane qualities that are difficult to explain by science. For example, how did she learn new languages, speak without opening her mouth, climb a wall, and levitate? She also distinctly knew when the nuns did and didn't put holy water on her food, and what items were blessed before they came to her.

The story of Anna Ecklund is so famous that in 2016, a movie based on her story was made called *The Exorcism of Anna Ecklund.* The movie depicts how horrible Anna felt during her experiences and how much the exorcisms impacted her. However, no matter how much the film showed these horrible acts, many believe that it is still not as traumatic as what the real-life Anna experienced.

4

BILL'S STRANGE ENCOUNTER

THIS STORY CENTERS ON BILL VAILE, a robotics engineer who worked at NASA for fifteen years. He was known as a pragmatic person. People described him as being to-the-point and factual—a traditional man of science. At NASA, he worked with the nuclear submarine service and was an expert on sonar. He also worked in the aerospace electronics and consumer electronics manufacturing fields, and was an operational manager (The Defectives Podcast, 2017). He was highly regarded at his job and well respected. However, Bill's life changed when he began to experience the paranormal.

The story of Bill's encounter is an interesting one, as it stumps paranormal skeptics. This is because Bill was a scientist, understanding reality consists of observable, testable, peer-reviewed data. Usually, those who staunchly believe in science do not believe in the supernatural Therefore, this type of story is rare. Additionally, Bill's story is corroborated by other people, which is always helpful when attempting to prove that something is true. No matter what you believe, the story itself is a great exploration of the supernatural.

The Life of Bill

Bill's story began in 2002 when he and his wife separated, and he moved back to his hometown of Arlington, Texas to recuperate, regroup, and figure out his next steps. He moved into a new home and worked with his little brother at his water purification company. Here, his job was to go into customer's homes and explain how to install and use the purification system. He began working on Saturdays and was sent to jobs by the main dispatch line, which would give him addresses and some details about the person he was helping. Though different from his life with NASA, this was likely a good change of pace for Bill and took him all over Arlington to assist with people's issues.

On one Saturday, Bill received a message from dispatch advising that he was needed at a home, and that the customer was very specific about his arrival time. He needed to be there at five o'clock, and was not to be late, but was also not to be early. Though this was unusual, Bill still attended the property, thinking nothing of it. Bill arrived at the house at one minute to five and was shocked by what he found. The customer was a woman who immediately started screaming and shouting when he arrived. As he approached, the woman yelled, "Get out of here!" Bill also heard her speaking in tongues. Accounts vary on what happened next, as some say that Bill fled the home immediately, fearing this woman would hurt him, while others claim Bill approached further and saw three men on their hands and knees, with the woman standing above them, commanding that an unknown spirit leave the men alone. Reportedly, the door then slammed on Bill and he left the property. Whichever story is true, the incident was enough to scare Bill, and he went home with a feeling that something was not right.

The Paranormal Begins

That night, Bill was relaxing after his difficult day and watching television with the lights in his house off when he noticed something skidding across the floor of the living room from the corner of his eye. Bill was alone in the house, didn't have any pets, and had never spotted mice or rats, but naturally assumed one had gotten into the house and searched for it. After he found nothing, he went to bed and planned to find it the next day. Once in bed and asleep, Bill felt the sensation of something running across his foot and woke in a panic. He turned the light on and, once again, looked everywhere for the rodent, but found nothing. He assumed that his mind was playing tricks on him and went back to sleep.

The situation was much worse when he woke up again. This time, he was woken by his bed violently shaking. Once he opened his eyes, the shaking stopped. As a rational man, Bill turned to the internet to see if there was any reason why this had happened. Most results showed it was likely that an earthquake was the cause, but Bill could not find any evidence of an earthquake hitting his hometown. His research showed that a military airbase was nearby, and that perhaps the shaking had come from something happening at the site. Midway through his search, Bill's internet cut out. That had never happened before.

Always the pragmatist, Bill reached out to the internet provider right away to get this fixed. When customer service put him on hold, he listened to the hold music. A static noise interrupted this, followed by a voice speaking in tongues, which sounded very threatening. Bill hung up the phone, and customer service called him back. When he reconnected with the same operator, he asked if the person on the other line heard the noises coming through. After a pause, the operator replied that they did. They could not figure out how this had happened, as they were on a secure line, but no further investigation followed.

Bill tried to go back to sleep, but thoughts of the occurrences that had happened to him that day plagued him. First the strange women, then the rodent, the shaking, and finally the unexplained voice over the phone. Just one of these events may be enough to cause a person to take pause, but four in one day was quite distressing for Bill.

As he lay there playing back the day, he heard something under his bed. He was sure that it had to be his mind messing with him, especially after a long, arduous day. He knew he wasn't thinking straight, but still was worried, as he couldn't figure out where the noise was coming from. Once he looked down to the foot of the bed, he saw a hand slowly reaching out from under the side. The hand attempted to grab his foot, but missed and pulled back under the bed. Bill was utterly terrified and turned on the lights in the room, then turned every light in the house on. He did not want to go back to sleep and stayed up all night in fear of what was happening to him.

Bill tried to brush these events off as nothing and continued with his life the next day as normal. When he got home and was having dinner, a glass bottle flew towards him and nearly hit him. Immediately after this, all the lights in his house went off. Bill grabbed a flashlight and walked around the house, trying to find the source of this act, when he heard something in one of his closets. He assumed that this was someone hiding in his home. He called his brother over immediately and asked him to check the closet. His brother, Bob, was as pragmatic as Bill, and the two went to check out the noise, thinking it was an intruder. Bill was still quite shaken, so he asked his brother to go to the closest. When he did, Bob felt something first hit his leg, then hit him in the face. Bob does not know what happened to him, but did not see anyone in the closet.

The brothers called their friend Michael, a sound engineer, for further assistance. They wanted another level-headed person to help them figure out what was happening in the house. While on the phone with Michael, Bill once again heard the demonic voice that had been present during his call with the customer service operator. Michael quickly plugged in his sound equipment to record, but Bill did not think this was a good idea. He was overcome with a bad feeling and told Michael to stop. Once Michael stopped, the voice disappeared, and they could hear nothing on the recorded audio.

Feeling unsafe in the house alone, Bill asked Bob to stay, and they invited Bob's wife Cindy to come over for dinner. During dinner, Bill once again saw the rodent-type animal running across the room. Bill asked his brother to swap chairs. When they did, Bob also saw the creature, though it is believed that he saw something running on two feet, unlike any animal he knew. Cindy also glimpsed it. The couple suggested calling animal control, but Bill was beginning to believe that this was beyond the regular issues people experienced. He looked into the paranormal to explain what was happening in his home.

Paranormal Investigators and Paranormal Escalations

Bill's research brought him to Brian Hall, a paranormal investigator. He found that Brian and his team approached their research scientifically and felt comforted by this. They came over and immediately began capturing the strange and scary incidents that were happening in the house. As they watched the footage, they saw a mist forming across the room from no source. The mist swirled in front of a laser the team had set up, but they could not be sure what this was and what this meant. Brian and his team were not sure that anything paranormal was present in the house. Most of the time, he found that signs of the supernatural were more evident than what they were seeing. Nonetheless, they persevered in their search for more clues regarding what Bill had witnessed. Despite this, they were unable to determine that anything unusual was happening in the house and could not explain what Bill had witnessed. Brian was stumped and suggested that Bill leave the property, but Bill refused.

Though the investigators had found nothing, the torment did not end for Bill. Terrified of what was happening in the house, he kept all his lights on and sat with his knees tucked up against his chin. He also slept this way, worried that something would attempt to grab him again. Additionally, he played the radio by his bedside to distract himself from the goings-on in both his brain and in his home.

Before he could even get to sleep, another strange and frightening occurrence happened in his home. Whilst in bed, Bill heard a large crash, as though a truck had rammed into the side of his house. The sound was so deafening that Bill was sure it had to be something physically destroying his home. He immediately ran outside to check out the noise, but found absolutely nothing to explain it. There was no damage and no clues as to where the noise originated. Once he re-entered the house, he heard the same noise, though there were still no signs of what was causing it. As this happened, his car alarm also rang, and Bill felt as though he was losing his mind. This started becoming a nightly occurrence, and Bill was unable to sleep in his home, but did not want to leave.

One night, as the crashing sound happened, Bill screamed at the top of his lungs, both from exhaustion and trying to scare off whatever was causing this. On this night, the crashing noise moved to his bedroom. As he entered the room, it became completely silent. It was an eerie silence, not a comforting one. The next sound he heard was the sound of feet shuffling as something moved around under his bed. It was at this point that something finally emerged for Bill to see. It was a large, six-foot-tall figure which had a massive tooth coming out of its mouth. It moved towards Bill, who stood frozen, and put its face right up against his. It did no harm, and quickly disappeared after letting out a grunting noise.

Bill continued to see this horrible figure in his house, and it continued to cause havoc on his life, though Bill stopped challenging it. He saw this was not helping the situation. He continued to be tormented, and the situation escalated as the creature began to harm Bill physically. He would wake up with scratches all over his chest and even had to be hospitalized a few times. Bill even experienced heart attacks because of the extreme stress that he was under.

As the paranormal investigators could not help, Bill took research into his own hands and dedicated his time to finding all the information he could about demons and exorcisms. This led Bill to the first clue as to why this was happening to him. He recalled the strange experience he had had when visiting the home of the woman who needed assistance with her water purifier. He determined that the screaming that was coming from her house was because an exorcism was happening on the property. He believed that as the demon exited the host during the exorcism, it needed a new body to possess and planted itself in Bill. He recalled she had been very specific about the time that she needed him to arrive at her house, and assumed she had timed it so that when he got to the property, the demon would leave the original host and enter him. Though he could not prove this, it was the only answer he had to what could be happening to him. It made sense, as this was when his problems all started, and many of the paranormal events seemed demonic in nature.

Where is Bill Now?

Though he sought to oust the demon from both his home and his body, Bill was ultimately unsuccessful and continued to live with this torment for many years to come. When asked why he wouldn't leave, he would answer that he didn't want to put somebody else through the hell he was going through. He worried that the sale of the house would mean the demon stayed there, and he could never live with himself if someone else had to experience this because of him. He tried numerous times to rid the house of the demon; he had exorcists, paranormal investigators, and religious groups visit, though none of these tactics were successful. For almost two more decades, Bill remained at the house.

There are many reasons to be skeptical of Bill's story, and those who do not believe in the paranormal have theorized that this is all either a fabrication or that his mind really was playing tricks on him and that he believed that something was happening. First, there is very little physical proof that there was something haunting his home. No photos or videos were concrete enough to show that there was a spirit, and ultimately, even the eyewitnesses' stories could be discredited. The only people who witnessed what was happening were Bill's immediate family, and they are sometimes viewed as subjective audiences to such incidents.

Ultimately, there is also a lot of reason to believe Bill. First, we should remember that he is a man of science who worked with NASA for fifteen years and was a well-respected member of their staff. He exhibited no traits that would lead people to believe that he was a liar or someone who would imagine the paranormal, and was even skeptical of the situation himself when it first started. Bill was not a believer, and only became one after the demon entered his home. Bill has also been psychically attacked by the demon and was hospitalized due to the torment. It is unlikely that these would be self-inflicted wounds, and this proves to be a solid piece of evidence in his favor. Further to this, Bob was also attacked in the home, and Cindy caught a glimpse of something there. There would be no concrete reason for these two people to lie and perpetuate this story further.

Though we may never know what is true, this story is still terrifying and is a fascinating insight into the different types of demons that could exist.

5

THE EXORCIST TRUE STORY: REAL CASE OF POSSESSION?

THE ORIGINS OF THE OUIJA BOARD ARE ALMOST AS MYSTERIOUS as the supernatural pronouncements the device is said to conjure. Now a staple of sleepovers and summer camp high jinks, the modern version can trace its beginnings to the nineteenth century, when the first advertisements for the Ouija appeared in newspapers across the Eastern United States.

The demand for such a device came from a growing interest in contacting the spiritual world, resulting in several iterations of 'talking boards' being marketed to those interested in communicating with the dead. This desire increased in the years after the US Civil War, as family members hoped to communicate with loved ones they had lost. Even Mary Todd Lincoln, the wife of President Abraham Lincoln, used spiritualism—the theory that it is possible for the living to communicate with the dead—to contact her son William. Unfortunately, the latter had died at the age of eleven due to fever.

By 1890, Elijah Bond was credited with patenting the design that matches the current one, featuring the alphabet, numbers zero to nine, and the words 'yes', 'no', and 'goodbye'. He also patented the planchette, the teardrop instrument used to move about the board.

Although most saw it as a simple parlor game, the Ouija and its intended results grew in popularity; so much so that it soon caught the ire of the Catholic Church, who went so far as to ban their use. Bans from other Christian sects followed this, who saw it as a pathway towards evil. Unfortunately, when we consider the stories that follow, it seems they may have been right.

Roland

It was the late 194os. Roland Doe was described as a normal thirteen-year-old boy living in Cottage City, Maryland, a suburban community outside Washington, DC. When his story broke, to protect his anonymity, he was given the pseudonym of Roland or Robbie Doe. The only child in a devout Lutheran home, Doe was a lonely child. Although details are sketchy, his family life seems to have been highly dysfunctional. The one constant in his life was his Aunt Harriet (sometimes referred to as 'Hattie' or 'Tillie'), who was a spiritualist who believed it was possible to communicate with the deceased.

Harriet taught her nephew how to use an Ouija Board to contact the 'other side'. Devoted to his aunt, Doe doted on her, his only friend in a lonely world. A world that would become less structured when, in early 1949, his aunt died from complications with multiple sclerosis. In an attempt to contact his late aunt, Doe used the techniques he'd learned and allegedly put his Ouija to use. This thought is somewhat controversial because the strange phenomena that would befall Doe began on January fifteenth, 1949, and his aunt's death did not occur until January twenty-sixth.

Whatever the timeline, the events that would follow would be the catalyst for William Peter Blatty's 1971 novel The Exorcist and the film that followed two years later.

Strange Activity

Whether or not Doe attempted to contact his late aunt by using a Ouija, the next several months would contain an astounding sequence of unexplained events. The series of peculiar occurrences began throughout the family's home, often coinciding with the times Doe entered a room. To begin, a jumble of strange and unexplainable noises could be heard from different parts of their home. These included footsteps, often at night in parts of the house that the family knew were empty, and strange scratching and rapping noises emanating from behind the walls. Logically, it was first thought to be mice or some other infestation. However, when the family hired an exterminator to investigate the matter, their search turned up no evidence of vermin.

What happened next was even more unsettling. Furniture, dishware, and appliances inexplicably changed location in different rooms, usually following Doe's departure from that part of the house. The family's fears intensified when these occurrences began to happen right before their eyes. Items would levitate or be hurled across the room by a seemingly invisible force, water dripped from pipes that were in perfect working order, and Doe's bed—mattress and all—would shake nightly.

Knowing of her late sister's propensity for spiritualism, Doe's mother, accompanied by his grandmother, attempted to perform a ritual to determine if it was indeed Harriet who was causing these phenomena to happen. At first, she asked Harriet to knock three times to confirm it was her. At this point, a wave of cold air wafted over her, Doe, and his grandmother. As requested, they heard three knocks. But when they posed the question again, four knocks followed.

Around the same time, Doe began to exhibit unusual behavior. Mysterious marks and scratches appeared on his body. At school, inanimate objects would move whenever in the vicinity of Doe, disturbing his fellow students. Neighbors reported hearing screams and other terrifying noises coming from the house. A darkness seemed to follow Doe everywhere he went, which is a crucial aspect of his story. The incidents outside the home eliminated any theory that these episodes were caused by a poltergeist or ghost explicitly tied to the house's location. It also led his parents to theorize that the Ouija paved the way for a demon to possess their son's body.

Exorcism

After concluding that there was more at stake than ghostly manipulation, Doe's parents sought help from their local pastor, Reverend Luther Schulze, and an area psychiatrist. Doe was thoroughly examined at Georgetown University Hospital, only to be found healthy and psychologically sound. Then, on the advice of Pastor Schulze, Doe spent a night at the pastor's home so he could get a better understanding of the situation. One night was all it took for the pastor to recommend Doe's parents contact a Catholic priest by the name of Edward Hughes to perform an exorcism. This would be Hughes' first attempt at an exorcism, and it soon became clear that it would fail.

Tied to his bed, Doe began convulsing profusely. He exhibited what was described as "inhuman strength", freeing his arms and legs and attacking the priest. Doe was said to have torn a spring from the bed and used it to inflict an injury to Hughes' arm. Overwhelmed, Hughes ceased the exorcism and suggested the family seek the help of a more experienced priest.

It was at this time that yet another inexplicable development occurred. Gashes appeared on Doe's body, including one that spelled out "St Louis". His mother, who was from the midwestern city, immediately took it as a sign and the family traveled to a relative's home in St Louis. There, they would seek the help of Father Raymond Bishop, who, along with Father William Bowdern, would start their investigation.

Almost immediately, the two priests bore witness to many of the same peculiarities seen in Maryland. Objects near Doe were flung across the room. His aggressiveness and physical strength were now accompanied by a demonic voice that seemed disgusted with anything holy or Christian. Though this was only the priests' first visit with Doe, Bishop and Bowdern felt they needed more evidence and received permission from the local archbishop to begin the exorcism. Doe's real fight was about to begin.

The first exorcism rituals lasted over two months and occured at the home Doe was visiting and at a St Louis hospital. The process would include several priests—mostly Jesuits—including Father Walter Halloran, who insisted that several witnesses be present. In addition, Bishop would keep detailed logs, as did a member of the hospital's psychiatric staff. Thanks to these witnesses, much of what would play out would be recounted in Blatty's book and seen in the 1973 movie.

Like the fictional Regan MacNeil, Doe shouted profanities at the priests in an unnatural voice, taunted them, and threw tantrums. It was clear that the force which had taken hold of Doe was doing everything it could to derail the exorcism.

Witnesses, in particular Halloran, wrote of the bed shaking uncontrollably, Doe speaking in Latin, and dark marks inexplicably appeared on his body, spelling out the word 'evil'. In the struggle's culmination, Doe broke Halloran's nose, drawing blood. All told, over thirty rituals were conducted on Doe.

In the end, the exorcists triumphed, liberating the boy from his demonic intruder. One witness' account said that Doe screeched one last time during the final ritual, then collapsed on the bed. A strange, sulfuric odor permeated the room and dissipated. Roland Doe was free of his tormentor.

What Happened to Roland Doe?

Doe and his family would return to Maryland, where he would continue his life unencumbered. While there were many rumors regarding Doe's life following the events in St Louis—everything from committing suicide to becoming an airline pilot or working for the US government—the truth was far less notable. In fact, his life became fairly normal following his ordeal. As a teen, he would convert to Catholicism and attend Catholic high school. Later, he would marry and become the father of three children. This relative obscurity may have been purposeful. His parents offered little information about the incident in the years that followed, and it is said that Doe had little memory of what took place. This led to discrepancies in the story, fueled by media reports which created confusion over what was true and what had been blown out of proportion.

Some skeptics have downplayed the theory of demonic possession, saying an imaginative teenage boy out to cause mischief and bring attention to himself could explain everything that happened—a theory that came from Doe's alleged lonely upbringing. Still, others from the psychiatric profession believe it may have been a mental health issue and could be explained as an episodic event. But until their dying days, none of the principal religious players in this saga ever refuted what they saw as anything less than demonic possession.

CONCLUSION

AS WE COME TO THE END OF THIS SPINE-TINGLING COLLECTION OF TALES, it's time to contemplate the enigmatic threads that have woven themselves into the very fabric of these narratives.

Throughout these stories, we've witnessed the extraordinary manifestations of the supernatural. From Bill Vaile's inexplicable encounters in Arlington, Texas, to Jackie Hernandez's eerie experiences in San Pedro, California, the mysteries of the Nahanni Valley in Canada, and Anna Ecklund's harrowing exorcism, we've been left with a profound sense of the unexplained and the paranormal.

The people who graced these pages brought their unique perspectives and experiences, breathing life into these accounts. Bill Vaile's transformation from a rational NASA scientist into a believer is a striking example of human adaptation in the face of the extraordinary. Anna

Ecklund's story, marked by her resilience and the mysterious nature of her experiences, challenges conventional explanations and demonstrates our ability to evolve in the presence of the unknown.

These narratives have evoked emotions, from the heart-wrenching moments of Anna Ecklund's possession to the chilling encounters with the supernatural in the San Pedro Affair and Bill Vaile's terrifying ordeals. Together, they have offered a gripping exploration of the unknown and the intricacies of the human psyche.

"Creepy Paranormal Stories" reminds us that ghost stories extend beyond entertainment. They draw attention to unexplained tragedies affecting individuals and families. As we conclude the book, let's reflect on the emotions and thoughts these stories evoke. Whether we ponder the boundary between skepticism and belief in Jackie Hernandez's "San Pedro Affair" or savor a well-crafted tale, may these words continue to resonate with us after we've finished reading.

Thank you for embarking on this literary journey through "Creepy Paranormal Stories." While the stories may conclude here, the impact they've left upon us will endure.

REFERENCES

Clune, B. (2017). Hollywood Obscura : death, murder, and the paranormal aftermath. Schiffer Publishing Ltd.

Dobson, J. (2018, April 14). The Queen Mary Opens Up Its Haunted Hotel Suite For An Overnight Ghostly Experience. Forbes. https://www.forbes.com/sites/jimdobson/2018/04/14/the-queen-mary-opens-up-its-haunted-hotel-suite-for-an-overnight-ghostly-experience/?sh=21d9f942575b

Fahrlander, C., & Vickers, N. (2020, October 30). Haunted Heartland: The Sallie House in Atchison, KS. KCTV Kansas City. https://www.kctv5.com/news/local_news/haunted-heartland-the-sallie-house-in-atchison-ks/article_f0ad791a-1a26-11eb-bff6-4382ee261acb.html

Fyfe, D. (2014). Overland Limited. The Campo Santo Quarterly Review, 1(4). The Campo Santo. https://www.camposanto.com/quarterlyreview/volume-1/issue-4/overland-limited/

Jones, J. (2011, October 30). San Diego landmark is ghost hunters' old haunt; Whaley House, an 1850s residence rich in history, is known for its alleged spectral encounters, which tend to increase in late October. The Los Angeles Times.

Kroonenberg, S. (2013). Why Hell Stinks of Sulfur : Mythology and Geology of the Underworld (A. Brown, Trans.). Reaktion Books.

Lawrence, A. (2017). Paranormal survivors: Validating the struggling middle class. Journal of Popular Film and Television, 45(4), 219–230. https://doi.org/10.1080/01956051.2017.1302922

Maysh, J. (2019, November 16). The Murder House. Medium. https://medium.com/s/story/the-murder-house-8bea26f11e5b

Miller, V. (1873, October 7). Hanging Yankee Jim. Los Angeles Herald. Hanging Yankee Jim

Monif, M. (2020, October 20). A disease often misdiagnosed as madness. Monash Lens. https://lens.monash.edu/@medicine-health/2020/10/20/1381554/autoimmune-encephalitis-when-your-body-attacks-your-brain-and-people-think-youre-going-mad

Naval Historical Society of Australia. (1998, September 18). SS Queen Mary & the loss of HMS Curacoa 1942. Naval Historical Society of Australia. https://www.navyhistory.org.au/ss-queen-mary-the-loss-of-hms-curacoa-1942/

Paynter, S. (2021, July 9). Inside the infamous "Murder House" embroiled in new mystery. New

York Post. https://nypost.com/article/inside-loz-feliz-murders-house-harold-perelson/

Pickman, D. (2010). The Sallie house haunting : a true story. Llewellyn.

Pool, B. (2009, February 6). On a Los Feliz hill, murder — then mystery. Los Angeles Times. https://www.latimes.com/archives/la-xpm-2009-feb-06-me-mansion6-story.html

Richardson, A. (2019). Sign the Petition. Www.change.org. https://www.change.org/p/the-queen-mary-and-epic-entertainment-group-change-the-background-story-of-half-hatch-henry-at-queen-mary-s-dark-harbor?source_location=petitions_browse

Strudwick, J. A. (1960). The Thomas Whaley House. Historical Shrine Foundation Of San Diego County.

The Queen Mary. (n.d.). Queen Mary Story - TheQueen Mary - Legendary Queen Mary Ship in Long Beach. Www.queenmary.com. Retrieved August 14, 2021, from https://www.queenmary.com/history

Wilson, C. (2000). Afterlife. Caxton.

DREAD: THE UNSOLVED Takes on the Exorcism of Michael Taylor. Dread Central, 3 June

2021. www.dreadcentral.com/news/401927/dread-the-unsolved-takes-on-the-exorcism-of-michael-taylor/.

Bishop, Fr. R. J. (2019, Oct. 19) The Actual 1949 Diary of the Priest Who Inspired the 1973 Film: The Exorcist. Sensus Fidelium. https://sensusfidelium.us/the-actual-1949-diary-of-the-priest-who-inspired-the-1973-film-the-exorcist/

DeLong, W. (2017, Oct. 26) The True Story of Roland Doe That Inspired 'The Exorcist'. All That's Interesting. https://allthatsinteresting.com/roland-doe-the-exorcist-true-story

Hollingsworth, A. [Put the Shovel Down] The Horrifying Case of Michael Taylor (Demon or Bipolar Psychosis?) [Video] YouTube. https://www.youtube.com/watch?v=3MrNhHu-90w

Iggulden, C. (2017) The Exorcist Files. The Sun, Feb. 14, 2017.

McRobbie, L.R., The Strange and Mysterious History of the Ouija Board. Smithsonian, Smithsonian.com, 28 Oct. 2013. www.smithsonianmag.com/history/the-strange-and-mysterious-history-of-the-ouija-board-5860627/

Popcorn, Detective. The Possession of Michael Taylor. Last Podcast on the Left Reading List, 28 Oct. 2018. lastpodcastontheleftreadinglist.com/michael-taylor/

Taylor, T. (2014) The Devil Came to St. Louis, The True Story of the 1949 Exorcism (2nd ed.). Whitechapel Press.

Printed in the USA
CPSIA information can be obtained
at www.ICGtesting.com
LVHW020815040224
770879LV00038B/1295